D1226400

VICTORY IN EUROPE

VICTORY

EUROPE

IN

THE FALL
OF HITLER'S
GERMANY

EDWARD F. DOLAN

FRANKLIN WATTS ■ 1988
NEW YORK ■ LONDON ■ TORONTO ■ SYDNEY

Cover photograph courtesy of Sovfoto

Photographs courtesy of: FPG: p. 16; U.S. Army: pp. 28, 47,
61, 67, 104, 146; Imperial War Museum: pp. 42, 89; Heinrich
Hoffmann, *Life* Magazine, © Time, Inc.: p. 69; Library of
Congress: p. 76; UPI/Bettmann Newsphotos: pp. 94, 129, 144;
AP/Wide World Photos: p. 116; Tass from Sovfoto: p. 132

Maps courtesy of Vantage Art, Inc.

Library of Congress Cataloging-in-Publication Data

Dolan, Edward F., 1924–
Victory in Europe.

Bibliography: p.
Includes index.
Summary: Surveys the final months of World War II
in Europe, including the Battle of the Bulge, the
liberation of the death camps, the execution of
Mussolini, the Yalta Conference, Germany's surrender,
and the death of Hitler.
1. World War, 1939-1945—Europe—Juvenile
literature. [1. World War, 1939-1945—Europe]
I. Title.
D755.6.D65   1988   940.54′21   87-20786
ISBN 0-531-10522-9

CONTENTS

1417427

VICTORY IN EUROPE

INTRODUCTION

The final months of World War II in Europe rank among the most memorable in history. Marking the close of one chapter in the greatest and—in terms of the lives sacrificed—most costly war ever fought, they were months that witnessed six great dramas:

The military actions that ended with the Allied nations destroying the once mighty and proud Germany.

The ignominious last days of Germany's Adolf Hitler as he crouched, like a trapped animal, in a concrete bunker beneath his capital city, Berlin, and finally took his own life.

The sudden death of America's wartime leader, President Franklin D. Roosevelt, of a cerebral hemorrhage.

The execution of Hitler's close ally, Italian dictator Benito Mussolini, at the hands of his enemies.

The political agreements that altered the geography of Germany and other European areas for years to come—perhaps even for all time—and led to the first meeting of the international peace organization, the United Nations.

The freeing of the prisoners in Hitler's concentration camps by Allied troops. News photos of the prisoners and the awful conditions in the camps brought to the world a full realization of the atrocities that so many of Europe's people, especially its Jewish population, had suffered during his reign.

The dramas of those final months played a vital role in an even larger drama. They were part of a great turning point in history. They contributed to the end of the world as it had once been and helped to usher in the vastly different world in which we now live.

Just how different is our world today from the world of the prewar years? Just three of many examples tell the story.

First, ours is a world of scientific marvels that had their initial uses in World War II. Among them are rockets and jet aircraft. The jet was seen for the first time above the battlefield in the final months of the European fighting.

Next, ours is a world of nuclear weapons that can be traced back to the German-American race to develop the atomic bomb. Germany lost the race when the Allied forces, moving in on her from all sides, began the final destruction of her military and industrial might. Had Germany, however, held out long enough and perfected the bomb ahead of the United States, Adolf Hitler might well have won the war's ultimate victory. If so, who now could guess what our lives would be like today?

And, finally, ours is a world of continuing conflict between the communist and free nations. Communism controls many areas today because of the ambitions of Russia's wartime leader, Joseph Stalin, and the political bargains he struck with his fellow Allied leaders in the last days of the war. But in the midst of all this conflict, ours is also a world that, through its United Nations, born in the last full month of the European fighting, tries to maintain international peace by having countries settle their problems with talk rather than arms.

Because the dramas that marked the close of World War II in Europe did so much to give us today's world, they should never be forgotten and, thus, are to be the subjects of this book. But, as much as these dramas deserve to be remembered by all, this book was not written simply to bring them to mind.

Quite as much, it was written with the overall hope that an understanding of the horrors of the war in Europe and of the ruthless dictatorship responsible for them will prompt us always to the work of safeguarding against a similar catastrophe in the future.

If the following pages succeed in realizing this hope, the book will have more than achieved its purpose.

CHAPTER

EUROPE
IN FLAMES

On September 16, 1944, Adolf Hitler met with three of Germany's leading military commanders and suddenly dreamed up a mighty attack for his armies. It would, he proclaimed, end World War II in Europe and bring him final victory over his Allied enemies.

It was a dream that came to nothing. In just seven months—at the dawn of May, 1945—it lay in ashes. By then, Hitler himself was dead by his own hand. By then, Germany had been reduced to ruins. And, by then, she was ending the European fighting not in the triumph that her Fuehrer had prophesied but in unconditional surrender.

In the following chapters, we're going to live through those seven months, from that meeting of September 16, 1944, to the day of surrender, May 7, 1945. They were months marked by one significant drama after another—in all, the six dramas that are described in the Introduction to this book. They ranged from decisive battles to the political agreements that changed the face of Europe.

They are dramas, however, that cannot be fully understood unless we know what went on before them. And so let us begin with a brief look first at the steps that led to World War II in Europe and then at the fighting it triggered.

THE ROOTS OF WAR

The steps leading to the war began in 1938 when dictator Adolf Hitler placed neighboring Austria under German control. The war was formally declared the next year by Great Britain and France as Hitler's armed forces invaded another of his neighbors, Poland. But the roots of what became the most monumental war, not just of the twentieth century but of all time, can be traced back to the end of World War I in 1918.

The costs of the First World War left Germany economically drained and countless people jobless. Her defeat by the Allied nations filled her with humiliation. When Hitler entered politics in 1921, he took advantage of these two factors to win the people over to his small National Socialist Party, which in time became known simply as the Nazi Party.

To soothe the feelings of humiliation, Hitler said that Germany had not been defeated in battle. Rather, in one speech after the other, he shouted the groundless charge that she had been the victim of traitors at home who had undermined the war effort. He further sought to rebuild the nation's pride by telling the Germans that they were members of a superior race—in his words, a "master race"—and thus should dominate such lesser humans as the Jewish and Slavic peoples, both of whom made up much of the European population.

Still further, Hitler promised to heal Germany's economic wounds and bring widespread employment by rebuilding the nation into the power she had once been. Finally, he vowed to take revenge on the European nations that had crushed her in the war.

Vast numbers of Germans responded to these promises by joining the Nazi Party or otherwise supporting its growth. The result was that within a few years, Hitler became one of Germany's most powerful politicians. In 1934, his power was such that he took dictatorial control of the government and gave himself the title *Fuehrer*. In English, the term means "leader."

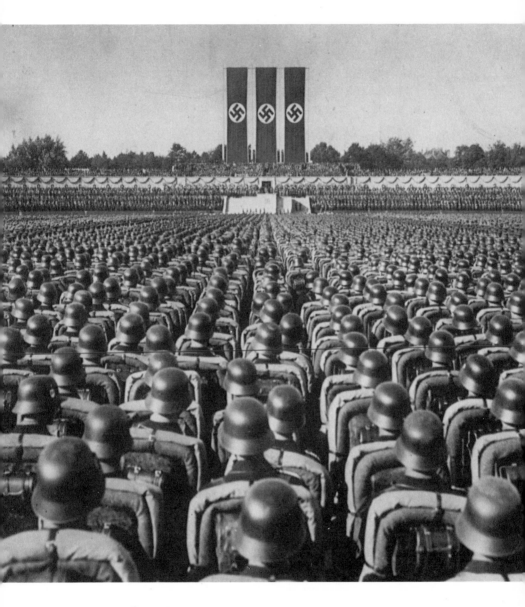

*At rallies such as this one in the 1930s, Hitler
fired the imagination and pride of his countrymen
with his vision of Germany's military power.*

Hitler kept his promises. He remolded Germany into an industrial power. He fashioned a huge army of splendidly trained infantry and panzer (tank) units; a navy boasting mighty battleships and fleets of hard-hitting submarines (called U-boats, meaning "underseas boats"); and an air force that was the greatest of the day. Then, in 1938, he began to expand Germany's territory with a series of political take-overs and military attacks. These led to the outbreak of World War II.

THE ROAD TO WAR

Austria was Hitler's first victim. He began his takeover by presenting the little nation with a treaty that would put her under Germany's thumb. He threatened an invasion if the country did not consent to his terms. Though Austria signed the treaty, her courageous Prime Minister later rejected it. Infuriated, Hitler ordered his troops into the country. Austria fell to him in March, 1938, without a single shot being fired.

The next victim was Czechoslovakia, a democratic nation that had been formed in the wake of the First World War. In the late summer of 1938, Hitler ordered the Czech government to give him the country's western region, which was known as the Sudetenland. He said that the area rightfully belonged to Germany because more than three million Germans lived there. The Czechs prepared to resist a promised invasion if the demand went ignored. An armed encounter was prevented when French, British, and Italian leaders—all hoping to avoid bloodshed—met with Hitler, agreed that he should have the Sudetenland, and forced the Czech government to surrender the region. In 1939, Hitler grabbed the remainder of Czechoslovakia.

That year of 1939 brought still another conquest. German troops flooded into Poland. Hitler knew that the invasion might provoke Great Britain and France into a declaration of war against him. Still exhausted from their losses in the First World War, they had no desire for a new conflict and had not opposed his Austrian and Czechoslovakian takeovers. But they had committed themselves to defend Poland should she be attacked. Were they to declare war, he feared that his longtime enemy, Russia, might join them. And so, to protect himself, he signed an agreement with Russia just prior to the invasion. In the agreement, which was called a nonaggression pact, the two nations promised not to fight each other.

Russian dictator Joseph Stalin, interested in expanding his country's power, took advantage of the pact to claim a slice of Poland for himself. He moved in soon after the German invasion, with the result that Poland's eastern area fell into Soviet hands while the western area went to Hitler. Stalin then demanded that several small countries nearby on the Baltic Sea give him military bases and certain territories. All but Finland bowed to his wishes. In November, he attacked the Finns. At first dazed by the stubborn and expert way their army fought back, Stalin finally drove them to surrender in early 1940.

And what of Hitler's attack on Poland? It was launched on September 1, 1939. The country, with its outnumbered and antiquated army, fell to him in little more than a month. As he had anticipated, the invasion triggered a declaration of war by Great Britain and France. The declaration came on September 3. Long feared by people everywhere, World War II was now a terrible reality in Europe.

THE WAR YEARS

Destined to last until 1945 and to be fought in Europe, Africa, Asia, and the Pacific, World War II eventually involved fifty-seven countries. Pitted against each other were the countries known as the Allied nations and those called the Axis powers. The largest of the Allied nations were, in alphabetical order, China, Great Britain (and its Commonwealth countries), the Soviet Union, and the United States. France is also listed as an Allied nation, but she fell to Germany in 1940 and, as a consequence, was unable to contribute a large body of men to the fighting. Those who fought for her were, in the main, Frenchmen who escaped the Nazi occupation.

The major Axis powers were Germany, Italy, and Japan. The smaller Axis nations included Bulgaria, Finland, Hungary, and Rumania (sometimes spelled Romania). The term *Axis* came from what was known as the Rome-Berlin Axis pact, a 1939 agreement in which Italy and Germany agreed to assist each other militarily and economically. Japan joined the pact in 1940.

Had you been alive at the time, you would have seen the war years bring the following march of events in Europe:

1940

In April, Hitler invades Norway so that the Norwegian seaports can not be used by the Allies to intercept the flow of needed steel for his war machine from neutral Sweden. Simultaneously, he attacks and conquers Denmark.

A month later, German forces sweep into Belgium, Luxembourg, the Netherlands, and France. The four countries fall quickly, with Germany's longtime archenemy, France, surrendering in June.

Hitler looks west across the English Channel and plans an invasion of Great Britain. In preparation, he unleashes a series of bombing attacks on the island nation. This action, which is soon called "The Battle of Britain," continues into 1941 and sees Hitler's *Luftwaffe* (air force) defeated by the Royal Air Force. The British invasion never takes place.

Italian dictator Benito Mussolini, long a Hitler ally, tries to conquer Egypt. When his forces are routed by the British army there, Germany comes to his aid. The Germans emerge victorious after a long series of battles that take the opposing armies all across the face of North Africa.

1941

Hitler, emboldened by his many successes, discards his nonaggression pact with Joseph Stalin and invades Russia. The attack on their homeland causes the Soviets to switch sides and join the allies. The Nazi invaders, at first thrusting deep into Russia, are eventually stopped at the cities of Moscow, Leningrad, and Stalingrad. The invasion will come to a dismal end in early 1943.

As part of his assault on Russia, Hitler drives the Soviet troops out of the western area of Poland, which they had taken during his 1939 invasion. Far to the south, he conquers Yugoslavia and Greece to help open an avenue into Russia's underbelly.

Once Hitler attacks Russia, Finland joins the Axis cause. The Finns take this step in the hope of receiving German help in freeing their country from their Soviet captors.

On December 7, the Japanese attack the United States at Hawaii's Pearl Harbor. Until now, the United States has remained neutral in the war, though providing the Allied nations with arms and other supplies. On December 8, President Roosevelt declares the United States to be at war with Japan. Germany and Italy declare war on the United States. Great Britain joins the United States in the Japanese war. Also aligned against Japan is China. The two countries have been at war since the Japanese invaded China in 1937.

1942

A British-American force invades North Africa to drive out the German and Italian forces there. The operation ends in victory for the invaders.

In July, following their North African triumph, the Allies attack the Axis forces on the island of Sicily, which lies just below the southern tip of Italy. The attack, which drives the enemy from the island by mid-August, is a prelude to an invasion of Italy itself.

Knowing that their country is soon to be attacked, the political foes of Italian dictator Benito Mussolini overthrow him and replace his regime with a new government. The new government quickly surrenders to the Allies. Italy drops out of the war, but the German troops there vow to fight on.

Though Italy is out of the war, the Allies nevertheless launch their invasion in early September, landing at the Gulf of Salerno on the southwestern coast. The next twenty months see them push the German troops slowly but steadily northward until the country is completely in Allied hands.

Nineteen forty-three also sees the German invasion of Russia at last fail for good. The Soviets begin a massive campaign to regain their lost territory and then advance on Germany itself.

1944

Allied armies, under the command of General Dwight D. Eisenhower of the United States, launch a major invasion of western Europe on June 6, a date that goes down in the history of the war as D-Day. The troops come ashore on the French west coast and, in the next months, move across France and spear northward into the Netherlands, Belgium, and Luxembourg.

On August 15, a major Allied force lands in southern France and begins to fight its way north to join the D-Day troops. In the meantime, the Russians continue to regain their lost territory and finally burst into Poland on the road to attacking Germany's eastern border.

By September, Hitler's Germany is threatened from two directions. The Allies are fast closing in on his borders from east and west. The closing months of World War II in Europe and the destruction they will wreak on Germany are at hand.

It is in that September of 1944 that our story begins.

CHAPTER

CODE NAME:
AUTUMN FOG

Adolf Hitler was living and working at his army headquarters in the latter half of 1944. It lay deep in the forests of East Prussia, a German area bordering northern Poland and separated from Germany itself by a wide strip of land. Consisting of concrete buildings and protected by barbed wire fences and heavily armed guards, the headquarters was called the *Wolfsschanze*, meaning, in English, "Wolf's Lair."

On the morning of September 16, at the end of a meeting with the headquarters staff, Hitler beckoned four of his top officers to one side. He said that he wanted to talk with them in private and would meet with them in a few moments. The four were Field Marshal Wilhelm Keitel and Generals Alfred Jodl, Heinz Guderian, and Werner Kreipe. With Keitel leading the way—as befitted his position as supreme commander of all German forces—the four went to a small room that was furnished with a few chairs and a desk on which was spread a map of Europe.

The officers talked quietly among themselves while awaiting Hitler's arrival. They wondered why the Fuehrer wanted to see them. Then, when he finally appeared, they studied him closely, just as they had studied him during the staff meeting and all through the past weeks. Now, as then, they did not like what they saw.

Hitler's face was pale. His mouth hung slack. The once-sharp blue eyes were watery and had a vacant look to them. Nodding a greeting, he crossed to the desk. He did not walk with his confident stride of old. Rather, with shoulders stopped, he dragged his feet along the carpeted floor. His right arm seemed to be hanging uselessly at his side.

THE MAN HE HAD ONCE BEEN

The four officers knew that they were seeing but the shadow of the man their Fuehrer had once been—the proud and ruthless politician who had become Germany's dictator, who had rebuilt the nation's armed might, and who had taken her to war. But they were not surprised by the change in him. The war, begun with so many glorious victories, had now become a disaster that was ruining his health. Germany was in mortal danger. Her enemies were pressing in on her borders from the east and west. Catastrophe was at hand. Hitler was cracking under the awful strain.

Along with the four officers, everyone stationed at *Wolfs-schanze* knew of Hitler's failing health. Everyone spoke of his blinding headaches, stomach cramps, and attacks of dizziness. Everyone saw how nervous he was and how stubbornly he was refusing to listen when his top military advisers said that all was lost and that surrender was the only way left to save Germany from complete ruin. There were whispers that he was losing his mind. These whispers seemed based on truth—expecially when he shrieked that the country must fight on to her every last man, woman, and child.

The four officers knew that Hitler was more than a sick man. He was also a wounded man. Less than two months ago—on July 20—a desperate attempt had been made on his life. Sure that he had gone mad and would not stop until he saw Germany destroyed, a group of officers had plotted to assassinate him. They had placed a bomb under a table where he was to stand during a staff meeting at the *Wolfs-schanze*. The bomb had been concealed in a briefcase and, on exploding, it had killed several officers, burned others, and left Hitler stunned, with his face blackened and his right arm hanging numb at his side. He had been spared death by the merest chance. An officer had accidentally kicked the case a few inches away from the Fuehrer and had saved him from the full blast of the explosion.

Hitler now dropped into a chair and stared up at the four officers. If he had not been insane before, they were sure that the assassination attempt had sent him over the edge. In a fury, he had ordered all his officers investigated. By the time the investigation ended, some five thousand were suspected of being involved in the plot. No matter who was guilty or not guilty, he had ordered them all executed.

Hitler sat slumped at the desk for a moment. Then, in a low, hoarse voice, he explained his reason for calling the four men together. He wanted their latest assessment of how the war was going. A nod told Colonel General Jodl to begin.

A SUDDEN CHANGE

As had been the case for weeks now, almost all of Jodl's news was bad. The Russian army was crashing toward Germany along the Eastern Front. Allied troops were pushing north-ward through Italy. The German divisions there would soon be driven out. On August 15, an Allied force had landed on the shores of southern France. It was spearing north to join the Allied troops that had been fanning out over France and into Holland, Belgium, and Luxembourg since the D-Day landings on June 6.

There was just one item of good news. The German troops in Holland were giving a good account of themselves. They had slowed the Allied advance there to a blood-soaked crawl.

Returning to the tragic side of things, Jodl reported that the army had suffered terrible casualties in the past three months—no fewer than 1.2 million men dead, wounded, or missing. More than half that number had fallen before the onslaught of the D-Day force as it fought its way from Normandy to the Siegfried Line, the great system of fortifications stretching along Germany's western border. The entire border was now threatened—from its southern end alongside France to the hilly and forested Ardennes area in the far north. It was but a matter of time before it gave way. . . .

The Ardennes! Surprised, the officers saw that one word trigger an abrupt and great change in Hitler. His look of exhaustion disappeared in an instant. He sat up straight. The sharpness of old filled his eyes.

They knew the reason for the change. The Ardennes, a heavily wooded area that stretched through eastern Belgium and Luxembourg to northeastern France, had been the scene of one of his greatest triumphs. In early 1940, his soldiers and tanks had blasted through its rugged terrain in the *blitzkrieg* attack that took them into France and ended with that longtime enemy in German hands. (*Blitzkrieg* means "lightning warfare" because of the speed with which the attack advances.) The French had been taken by complete surprise. They had never dreamed that he would strike from that direction because the Ardennes forests promised to make infantry and tank movements impossible. How wrong his daring had shown them to be!

The four officers had little time to be shocked by the change in Hitler. For now his hand came down hard and flat on the desk. He began to speak in a rush, pointing at locations on the map as the words tumbled out. Gone was his hoarseness of moments ago. His voice was clear and decisive—the voice heard in the better days of the war.

He had made a decision about the Ardennes this very minute, he said. It was now falling to the Americans, but it would soon be the scene of a new German victory—a victory far greater than the one of 1940. He would mass a group of armies along a section of the border there. He would loose them on a surprise *blitzkrieg* attack into Belgium and Luxembourg. They would smash through the American lines and spear their way to the Meuse River in Belgium. Then they

The concrete "dragon's teeth" of the Siegfried Line were designed to slow a tank assault on Germany's western border.

would advance on the combined British and United States troops in northwestern Belgium and take the city of Antwerp near the Dutch border. In true *blitzkrieg* style, they would move so quickly that the Allied commanders would have no chance to collect their wits and stop them.

With German forces controlling the land all the way to Antwerp, the attack would split the Allied forces on the Western Front into two halves. The troops in the north—in Holland and upper Belgium—would be cut away from their comrades to the south in lower Belgium, Luxembourg, and France. The split would achieve a wonder for Germany.

It would do no less than end the war in the West! Why? Because it would completely demoralize the enemy by showing them that Germany was far from beaten and had the strength and will to fight on for years to come. The British, exhausted by the long war, would give up and go home. The Americans were just as tired. They were also burdened with a war in the Pacific. They would quit Europe and concentrate on fighting the Japanese.

The triumphant German troops would then leave the West. They would join their comrades in the East and defeat the Russians. This would see the entire war at an end, with Germany victorious.

The plan seemed to be born on the spur of the moment. But General Jodl knew better. For weeks now, Hitler had talked with him of launching a massive attack that would somehow end the war—an attack that would take place in winter and thus make the fighting difficult for the British and American forces. Neither, in Hitler's opinion, was as rugged as his troops and would be at a great disadvantage in the cold. But he had never decided where to launch this offensive campaign. Now, in a split-second, he had made his choice.

Hitler's voice became more assured as he talked on. He spoke of Frederick the Great, the eighteenth-century Prussian king. Frederick had suddenly struck back at enemy

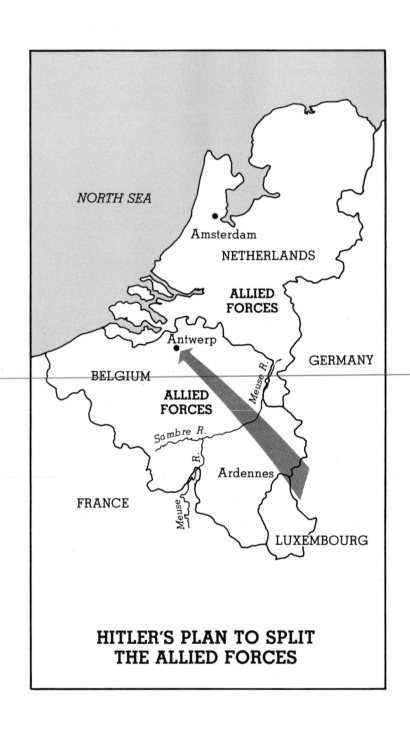

HITLER'S PLAN TO SPLIT
THE ALLIED FORCES

armies when facing certain defeat and had given Germany one of its greatest victories. The Ardennes attack would achieve just as fine a victory. The four officers listened with mixed emotions.

On the one hand, they felt that the British and the Americans could never be made to give up the war. They had it all but won. They would never run for home just because their forces had been split in one area. After all, they held thousands of square miles. They would simply regroup and drive forward. It was insane to think otherwise, though the four men dared not use that word in Hitler's presence these days.

But, on the other hand, the four could not help but be impressed by Hitler's enthusiasm. That enthusiasm had inspired countless people in the past and had driven them to follow him wherever he took them. Perhaps, though the thought seemed far-fetched—it could rally the German army to a final and complete victory. Who could tell?

Hitler's eyes swung to Jodl. The general heard the Fuehrer instruct him to draw up a detailed plan for the offensive. Though fearing that the winter would bring only disaster, Jodl nodded obediently and saluted.

OPERATION AUTUMN FOG

The next weeks saw Jodl carefully develop the plan. It went through several changes before achieving its final form. When completed, it called for Field Marshal Gerd von Rundstedt, the Commander-in-Chief of all German troops on the Western Front, to command the offensive. Von Rundstedt was to field three new armies. They were to be made up of men gathered together from other units. Side by side, the three were to thrust their way into Belgium and Luxembourg along an eighty-five mile front extending between two border towns—Germany's Monschau on the north and Luxembourg's Echternach on the south. Starting from the northern end of the front, the three armies were:

1. The Sixth SS Panzer Army, commanded by Colonel General Josef "Sepp" Dietrich.

    NOTE: In German, SS is the abbreviation for *Schutzstaffel*, meaning "guard detachment." The SS dated back to Hitler's early days in politics, when its men served as his personal army of bodyguards. In World War II, the SS was made up of elite units known for their toughness and deep loyalty to Hitler and the Nazi cause.

    The Sixth SS Panzer Army was to attack along the northern end of the front—between Monschau and the Losheim Gap; the Gap was a valley that extended some seven miles into Belgium from the German border. The Army was made up of nine divisions. Four were panzer divisions. One was a parachute outfit that was to serve as a ground rather than an airborne unit. And four were infantry divisions manned chiefly by recruits and by men from various units that had been badly damaged in the fighting.

2. The Fifth Panzer Army, commanded by General Hasso von Manteuffel. Responsible for the center area of the front, it was to attack along a line from the Losheim Gap south to the town of Wiltz. The Fifth also consisted of nine divisions—four panzer outfits, one panzer-infantry unit, and four infantry divisions.

3. The Seventh Army, commanded by General Erich Brandenberger. Made up of infantry divisions only— five in all—it was given the job of handling the southern end of the front, from Wiltz to Echternach.

Altogether, the German armies would field 250,000 men, 1900 pieces of heavy artillery, and some 950 tanks. They would be backed by several divisions standing by in reserve in case needed.

The plan called for General Dietrich's Sixth SS Panzer

Army to lead the offensive because his section of the front lay closest to the Meuse River. General Manteuffel's Fifth Panzer was to come right behind him. General Brandenberger's Seventh would likewise move forward, but his main job was to protect Manteuffel's men. Once the Allies saw what was happening, they were sure to hit Manteuffel with forces sent up from France.

On Hitler's orders, Jodl worked out the plan in the greatest secrecy possible. Only a few trusted officers were told of his work. There were two reasons for this. First, of course, the attack had the best chance of succeeding if it came as such a surprise that it threw the Allies completely off balance. Second, ever since the July 20 attempt on his life, Hitler had been increasingly suspicious of everyone around him. In particular, he feared that some of his people might have turned traitor and might now be spying for the Allies.

Consequently, he shook his head when he saw the code name that Jodl had chosen for the offensive—"Christrose"—and immediately changed it to *Wacht am Rhein*, meaning "Watch on the Rhine." He said that, if some traitor got hold of Jodl's code name and passed it on to the Allies, it would sound mysterious enough to make them suspect that some sort of trouble was afoot. *Wacht am Rhein* sounded more like a plan for the defense of Germany along her great Rhine River. It stood a good chance of not arousing Allied suspicions.

The code name underwent a final change in the days just before the offensive was launched. It became "Autumn Fog." The name was an apt one. Heavy fog, joined with snow, was destined to play a major role in the offensive. For many long days, it would keep Allied aircraft from attacking the German forces and dropping needed supplies to the American ground troops.

THE FINAL STEPS TO ACTION

All did not go well as Autumn Fog moved into its final preparations. First, there was trouble from the man who was to lead the operation. Field Marshal von Rundstedt thought the

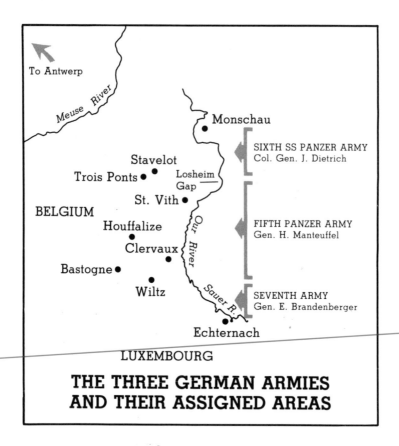

To Antwerp

Meuse River

Monschau

Stavelot

Trois Ponts ● ● Losheim
Gap

St. Vith ●

BELGIUM

Houffalize
●

Clervaux
●

Bastogne ●

Wiltz
●

Our River

Sauer R.

Echternach

LUXEMBOURG

SIXTH SS PANZER ARMY
Col. Gen. J. Dietrich

FIFTH PANZER ARMY
Gen. H. Manteuffel

SEVENTH ARMY
Gen. E. Brandenberger

THE THREE GERMAN ARMIES
AND THEIR ASSIGNED AREAS

attack was sure to fail. He said that it was being too hastily put together and that it had no chance of making the British and Americans quit the war. Another high-ranking officer, Field Marshal Walther Model, felt the same way. Both urged that lesser actions be staged—assaults that would damage the enemy and help to protect the German border against future advances. Hitler furiously rejected these ideas. Von Rundstedt had less and less heart for the plan as the days went by.

Second, Hitler had originally hoped to launch the attack sometime in early December. But the date had to be postponed several times because the job of forming the new armies and moving them up to the line was a tremendous one. Further, the movement was hampered by the snows and mists of what was proving to be the most severe European winter in years. Still further, everyone moved slowly so as to make as little noise as possible and not trigger the suspicions of the American troops just across the border. In many spots, planes flew overhead to keep the sounds of tanks rumbling into place from reaching the enemy foxholes. It was not until the night of December 15, 1944, that all was in readiness.

Autumn Fog would leave the planning stages and transform itself into a terrible reality with the coming dawn.

CHAPTER

THE BATTLE
OF THE BULGE:
DAY ONE

It was Saturday, December 16, 1944. The time was 5:29 in the morning. All was quiet at the American front-line posts stretching southward through the Ardennes for eighty-five miles (137 km) from Monschau to Echternach. Snow lay on the ground. A whitish mist filled the air. There was a strong wind in some areas. In others, a light rain was falling.

The officers and men, all members of the U.S. First Army, shivered in the forward posts and thought only of the bitter cold. The idea that they were about to face a full-scale attack never crossed their minds. Their front had been quiet and inactive for weeks now. Though they could clearly see the enemy over on the Siegfried Line with its many gun emplacements, hardly a shot was ever fired here.

There was fighting to their north and south. Up north, the U.S. Ninth Army was battling to take the Roer dams, which served Germany's great industrial area, the Ruhr. Assisting were units from their own First Army. Far to the south, the U.S. Third and Seventh Armies in France had smashed across the German border and were attacking another of Hitler's important industrial regions—the Saar. But here in the Ardennes, things were so quiet that the area was being called the "Ghost Front."

Likewise, all was quiet far to the rear. In camps dotting

west and northwest Belgium, much of the First Army was at rest after the weeks of fighting that had won the Ardennes.

Why was the Ardennes so quiet? Why did the men have no thoughts of an enemy assault? The answer to both questions was the same. The heavy forests made it especially difficult for an attacking force to maneuver. It was true that Hitler's troops had smashed through these forests and over these hills in 1940. But now his army was being beaten to a pulp. He did not have the strength to launch a major attack, much less one through this difficult region. Besides, who in his right mind would try anything in such miserable weather?

And so, all along the American line at 5:29 A.M. this bitter cold day of December 16, 1944, there was a feeling of calm at the American posts. One minute later, at 5:30, the quiet was shattered. Instantly gone were all thoughts that a German attack was out of the question.

Artillery shells of every description came pouring in from just behind the Siegfried Line. Some landed with the thump of mortar shells. Some came hurtling in from 88-millimeter guns and were known as "screaming meemies" because of the screeching sound that marked their approach. Some were fourteen-inch monsters fired from cannon mounted on railroad cars. And some were rockets shot from vehicle flatbeds. Exploding everywhere, the shells threw snow and dirt high, uprooted trees, severed communication lines, shattered command posts, and blasted foxholes into gaping wounds in the earth.

The massive attack was under way. The German soldiers who survived the next days would always remember it as the Ardennes Offensive. The Americans, because of the deep indentation it made in their lines, would call it the Battle of the Bulge.

THE TARGET AREA

Hitler could not have chosen a better spot for his offensive. The eighty-five-mile (137-km) front was lightly held by the

Allies because no one expected an attack here. Stretched along it were just six of the First Army's divisions. Five were infantry outfits, and one an armored unit. Starting at Monschau, they ran southward to Echternach in the following order: the 2nd and 99th Infantry Divisions (their units were mingled in some spots), the 106th Infantry, the 28th Infantry, the 9th Armored, and the 4th Infantry.

Three of the six divisions—the 2nd, 28th, and 4th—were veteran units exhausted from the weeks of fighting that had finally brought them here to the Ardennes. The rest were "green" units, all new to the war. They had been sent to the Ghost Front to accustom their men to battlefield conditions and light fighting before facing any heavy combat. Of their number, the 106th was the army's most recently formed division, while the 9th Armored had arrived in Europe just a short time ago and had been on the Ardennes front for no more than a week. In all, the six divisions numbered about seventy-five thousand men.

Massed over on the Siegfried Line were a quarter of a million men eager for battle. They had lived through months of humiliation as the Allies had driven the German forces steadily back across the face of Western Europe. A few moments ago, their commanders had read to them a message from Field Marshal Von Rundstedt. It was a brief but inspiring message that gave no hint of how little the Field Marshal actually thought of the impending offensive:

Soldiers of the Western Front! Your great hour has come. Large attacking armies have started against the Anglo-Americans. I do not have to tell you more than that. You feel it yourself. *We gamble everything!* You carry with you the holy obligation to give all to achieve superhuman objectives for our Fatherland and Fuehrer.

The message filled them with pride. At last, they were on the attack again. And those words: *We gamble everything!* It left no doubt as to the importance of the attack. It was meant to crush the Allies and save Germany from complete ruin. The future of their country lay in their hands. Now, as the shells flew overhead and blasted into the American lines, they stood ready to advance.

The bombardment lasted for about forty-five minutes. Then the guns fell silent. For the stunned Americans, the sudden quiet had an eerie quality to it. The stillness lasted but a few moments. Then came new sounds—the roar of tank and armored car engines starting up. Next, the figures of German infantrymen took shape in the mist. Charged with clearing a path for the tanks behind them, they wore white cloaks that made them hard to see against the snowy background. At the southern end of the front, the enemy lines were separated by a river that was called the Sauer along one stretch and the Our along another. Many of the Americans there heard the stamp of marching feet coming over the bridges that spanned the river. Some German troops rowed across in rubber boats.

Suddenly, at points along the front, enemy planes streaked in above the trees, flying past not with throbbing engines but with a deafening whine. They were jets, the latest of Germany's wartime developments. They were making their first appearance in battle. The German soldiers paused in surprise and looked up. A cheer broke from them. Their Feuhrer had given them a new miracle for this great battle. Then they continued their advance. Rifles began to crackle in the cold morning air.

DAY ONE: MIXED RESULTS

The purpose of the bombardment had not been to destroy the front-line posts. Rather, it had been aimed at disrupting the American communications system. It had succeeded. The American commanders were cut off from each other. Each did not know whether his fellow commanders were being attacked or whether his men alone were in trouble. Each

could not reach his headquarters for information and for orders as to how to coordinate with his fellow commanders to throw a counterattack against the Germans.

As a result, confusion reigned among the Americans throughout Day One of the battle. The stunned troops fought back as best they could. In some areas, behind-the-lines personnel—cooks, office clerks, truck drivers—grabbed rifles and were rushed forward to help their hard-hit comrades. At some posts, the green troops watched the advancing Germans in horror and then fled in search of safety. At others, they stood their ground and fought as hard as did the battle-hardened veterans elsewhere.

In general, despite the rampant confusion, the Americans—green troops and veterans alike—did well for themselves. Many successfully defended their posts while others fell back only after the hardest of fighting had almost wiped their units out. This stubborn defense, plus some problems on the opposite side of the line, gave the Germans mixed results on Day One of the offensive.

Each German army that day was to advance on targets between five and ten miles (8 and 16 km) from the Siegfried Line. Here, introduced by the map on page 44, is what happened to each.

The Sixth SS Panzer Army

General Josef Dietrich's Sixth SS Panzer Army, you'll recall, was to lead the offensive. Between Monschau and the Losheim Gap, he threw four of his divisions against the 2nd and 99th Divisions. His main Day One target was Elsenborn Ridge, the crest of a range of hills behind the American front lines. He felt certain that he would reach it without difficulty. The job would be especially easy because of the green 99th.

*Standing in front of an abandoned
U.S. Army tank, a panzer officer
shouts orders to his troops.*

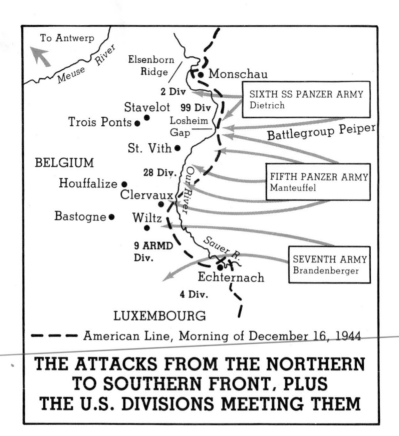

To Antwerp

Meuse River

Elsenborn Ridge

Monschau

2 Div

Stavelot 99 Div

Trois Ponts • Losheim Gap

SIXTH SS PANZER ARMY
Dietrich

Battlegroup Peiper

St. Vith •

BELGIUM

28 Div.

Houffalize •

Clervaux

Our River

FIFTH PANZER ARMY
Manteuffel

Bastogne • Wiltz

9 ARMD Div.

Sauer R.

Echternach

SEVENTH ARMY
Brandenberger

4 Div.

LUXEMBOURG

– – – American Line, Morning of December 16, 1944

THE ATTACKS FROM THE NORTHERN TO SOUTHERN FRONT, PLUS THE U.S. DIVISIONS MEETING THEM

He told his officers that its troops were sure to cave in quickly and run.

The General was wrong. Proving courageous—and inspired and helped by the 2nd Division veterans in their midst—the men of the 99th held fast. Dietrich's attack was slowed and, in places, stopped. At day's end, Elsenborn Ridge still lay beyond his grasp.

Farther south along Dietrich's front, there was another problem for the Germans. Autumn Fog called for a special force of more than one hundred tanks, accompanied by a fleet of armored cars, to smash through the Losheim Gap. The tanks were then to serve as a spearhead not only for Dietrich's army but for the entire offensive. Knocking the Americans aside and opening the way for the troops behind them, they were to dash forward and reach the Meuse River as soon as possible. From there, as planned, the offensive would be aimed at its final destination—the city of Antwerp.

Commanding the spearhead unit was Lieutenant Colonel Jochen Peiper. Dedicated to Hitler and the Nazi cause, Peiper had the deserved reputation of being a ruthless commander. On the Eastern Front, he had led a tank outfit known as the "Blowtorch Battalion." The unit had been given the nickname after burning two Russian villages to the ground and killing all their inhabitants.

Early on Day One, Peiper moved his force—which was called Battlegroup Peiper—up to the Siegfried Line for the thrust into the Losheim Gap. Swearing angrily, he found himself stalled in a massive traffic jam created by the thousands of soldiers and vehicles trying to get across the Line. He swung his tanks away and went searching for another crossover spot. As a result, the outfit was delayed for hours. Peiper did not arrive in Allied territory until late at night.

The Fifth Panzer Army

Going against the 106th and 28th Divisions, the diminutive General Hasso von Manteuffel (he stood just over five feet tall) met with better luck. Along with Dietrich, he was charged with attacking in the Losheim Gap. Some of his troops moved like lightning along the southern side of the Gap. Two reasons accounted for their speed. First, the area was the most lightly defended spot on the entire front. Only a few American units stood in their path and Manteuffel's troops quickly overwhelmed them, almost wiping one out. Second, the ground on this side of the Gap was less difficult than that faced by Dietrich's men on the opposite side.

The principal Day One target for the Manteuffel troops in the Gap was the village of Schoenberg. A short distance to their south, other Fifth Panzer outfits were crashing through the 106th Division's lines. Their target was also Schoenberg. When the two attacking forces met there, they would close the jaws of a pincer movement that would see the 106th completely surrounded. The division might fight on, but, trapped and held within a circle of German might, it would be of no good in the battle.

Once the 106th was surrounded and trapped, Manteuffel was to advance and take the city of St. Vith. It was an important target because of the main roads that ran out of it to the west, north, and south. The westward road would be used for a swift thrust into the heart of Belgium. All the roads would enable the Germans to bring up needed supplies with ease.

Farther south, Manteuffel was hitting the 28th Division. Though up against Americans still exhausted from the long battle to reach the Ardennes, some of his men were driven back. But others were surrounding the 28th's posts and heading for the town of Houffalize. Like St. Vith, it was important to the Germans because of the roads running out of it.

Still farther south, a heavy Manteuffel force was advancing along a main road to the town of Clervaux and meeting stiff resistance at various points. Once Clervaux was captured (it fell on Day Two), Manteuffel was to head for one of Belgium's most important cities—the rail and road center called Bastogne. With Bastogne's capture, the little general would have a clear run to the distant Meuse River—and then Antwerp.

The Seventh Army

General Erich Brandenberger's army, made up entirely of infantry units, moved as swiftly as the Fifth Panzer. Facing Brandenberger as he attacked in southernmost Belgium and northernmost Luxembourg were the 9th Armored Division and the 4th Division. Before the day was done, though encountering a stubborn resistance, his forces were swarming through the small villages in his area and joining the advance on Bastogne.

OPERATION *GREIF*

Lieutenant Colonel Peiper's spearheading tank force was not the only special German unit in the field on Day One. That

*U.S. Army engineers prepare to blow up a stretch
of Belgian railroad track in an effort to halt the
German advance in the Ardennes.*

day also saw another special unit cross the Siegfried Line and begin to infiltrate the United States front. To the Germans who saw it take off, it was an odd-looking outfit. Its men were dressed in American uniforms and carried American arms. Some of their number rode in American Jeeps.

The story of this unit dated back to the final days of planning for Autumn Fog. At that time, Hitler summoned a trusted SS officer—Lieutenant Colonel Otto Skorzeny—to *Wolfsschanze*. Skorzeny was an expert commando fighter, and Hitler told him that he had decided to add an extra wrinkle to the coming offensive—one that exactly suited the officer's commando talents. He instructed Skorzeny to search the armed forces for English-speaking soldiers and quickly organize them into a group that, dressed as Americans, would sneak through the United States lines. Once to the rear, they were to sabotage communications. They were to spread rumors of German victories and of American troops retreating in panic. They were to pass false orders and reports to the enemy commanders. In all, they were to breed as much confusion, fear, and havoc as possible.

Hitler gave their operation the code name *Greif*. In English, the word means "griffin." A griffin is a mythical animal that is usually half eagle and half lion.

Skorzeny went quickly to work. He was soon commanding a force of daredevils, coaching them in American slang and the use of American equipment. On Day One, he sent his men across the Siegfried Line at various points along the front. As matters turned out, only a few of them managed to work their way through the battle and arrive behind the lines. Others were captured and still others were wounded or killed in the fighting.

Despite losing most of its men on Day One, the operation proved to be a lasting headache for the Americans. *Greif* did some damage to United States defensive movements, especially on the day when the men in one of its Jeeps came upon some troops looking for the front and sent them up the wrong road. But by far its greatest harm was seen in the confusion that it triggered. Once the Americans learned that the enemy was working among them in disguise, they became deeply suspicious of each other. Much valuable time was lost whenever U.S. soldiers sighted someone unknown to them. The stranger's life was in danger until he could answer questions on subjects known only to an American—questions, for instance, on baseball and football statistics, movie stars, and Mickey Mouse cartoons. The Americans also protected themselves by using passwords (they were changed almost daily) on meeting each other. Death could follow in a moment if a stranger did not know the day's word. Such was the fate of a chaplain making his rounds among a string of foxholes one night.

Operation *Greif* ended in tragedy for its men who were captured. Because they were dressed in uniforms not of their own country, they were treated as spies rather than prisoners of war. The international rules of war, as set down by what are known as the Geneva Conventions, required that the lives of prisoners be protected but permitted spies to be executed. The *Greif* men were executed by firing squad.

DAY ONE ENDS

As the day passed, news of the attack filtered out of the Ardennes and began reaching the major American comanders. It was not until sunset that a report came into General Dwight D. Eisenhower's hands at SHAEF (Supreme Headquarters, Allied Expeditionary Forces) near Paris. Visiting him at the time was General Omar Bradley, the commander of the Twelfth Army Group. Because the communications lines from the front lines were still in disarray, the report was fragmentary and unable to indicate the true size of the attack. The two officers reacted to it in different ways.

Bradley saw the offensive as a "spoiling attack." You'll remember that, to the north of the Ardennes, the U.S. Ninth Army was battling for the dams on Germany's Roer River. Bradley thought the attack was meant to "spoil" the Roer operation by causing the Ninth to turn away and come down to help in the Ardennes.

Eisenhower disagreed. He felt that he was faced with a full-scale offensive and acted accordingly. He immediately called for help from the north and south of the battle zones. The 7th Armored Division was sent in from the Ninth Army in the north. The Third Army's 10th Armored Division was ordered up from the south. A few hours later, Eisenhower ordered the 82nd and 101st Airborne Divisions to the Ardennes from their distant camps in France and western Belgium.

General Courtney Hodges was the commander of the First Army and, as such, was in charge of the Ardennes region. When he first received the news that his six divisions there were being hit, he thought that he was likely up against a limited action, perhaps one designed to draw the Ninth Army away from the Roer River dams. Then, beginning to change his mind, he ordered a unit from his Army's 1st Division to head for the battle zone.

The orders from Eisenhower and Hodges set in motion the first of all the American outfits that would eventually be thrown into the Battle of the Bulge.

Deep in Germany, Adolf Hitler received reports of the battle through the day and into the night. Though his troops had been stalled or thrown back at points along the line, he was delighted with the way things were going. In general, his soldiers were advancing and would reach their objectives in the next days. At midnight, he called one of his generals on the telephone and exultantly shouted that the offensive was a success and that the war would soon be won.

The next days were to prove him dead wrong.

CHAPTER IV

THE BATTLE
OF THE BULGE:
THE TIDE TURNS

The fighting remained confusing at points along the front on Day Two, December 17. Despite the confusion, the offensive definitely took shape that day. It began to center itself on five major actions that were keys to a German victory. With some succeeding while others failed, they were to continue until late in the month.

The five actions are shown on the map below. We'll talk about each of them in turn as they raged from north to south along the front.

ACTION 1:

THE BATTLE AT ELSENBORN RIDGE

On December 17, the 2nd and 99th Divisions were still holding off General Dietrich's Sixth SS Panzer Army at the far northern end of the front. During the day, the two divisions began to retreat. They did not retreat, however, because they were being overwhelmed. Rather, fighting savagely every step of the way, they deliberately fell back to Elsenborn Ridge.

Lying about ten miles (16 km) from the Siegfried Line, the Ridge was a long stretch of hilltop that provided them with excellent defensive positions. They were immediately joined by men from two newly arrived units—the 1st Division outfit

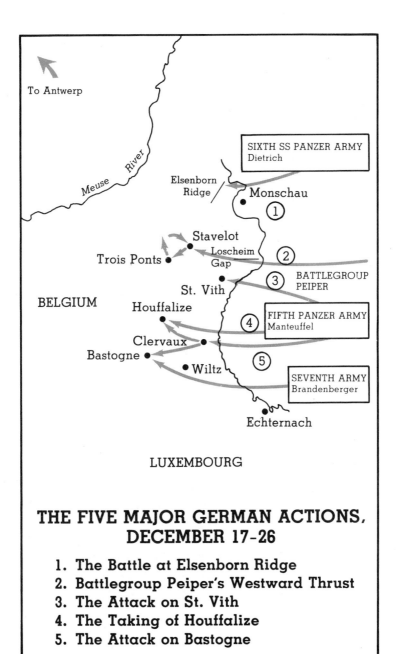

To Antwerp

Meuse River

SIXTH SS PANZER ARMY
Dietrich

Elsenborn
Ridge

Monschau

①

Stavelot

Loscheim
Gap

②

Trois Ponts

BATTLEGROUP
PEIPER

③

St. Vith

FIFTH PANZER ARMY
Manteuffel

BELGIUM

Houffalize

④

Clervaux

Bastogne

⑤

Wiltz

SEVENTH ARMY
Brandenberger

Echternach

LUXEMBOURG

THE FIVE MAJOR GERMAN ACTIONS, DECEMBER 17-26

1. **The Battle at Elsenborn Ridge**
2. **Battlegroup Peiper's Westward Thrust**
3. **The Attack on St. Vith**
4. **The Taking of Houffalize**
5. **The Attack on Bastogne**

that General Hodges had summoned, and troops from the 9th Infantry Division, which had been ordered in from the north a short time later. The Americans dug in and waited for the Germans to attack.

The attacks came immediately. Though suffering heavy casualties (the 99th alone lost two thousand two hundred men between December 16 and 20), the Americans successfully held their ground. By December 20, it was clear to a disappointed and infuriated Hitler that Dietrich's men were stopped dead in their tracks for good. The offensive at the northern end of the front had ended in failure.

ACTION 2:
BATTLEGROUP PEIPER'S
WESTWARD THRUST

To the south of Elsenborn Ridge, Dietrich's attack was proving more successful, with his units capturing American strongholds in and to the west of the Losheim Gap. The greatest success of all was being registered by the special tank force under Lieutenant Colonel Jochen Peiper. After being stalled the day before in heavy traffic, Battlegroup Peiper now broke into the clear. Up against just a few Americans, its more than one hundred tanks raced through the Gap and took the small town of Honsfeld.

Peiper's assignment, you'll recall, was to spearhead the Sixth SS Panzer Army's attack and, thus, the entire offensive. His orders were to drive hard at all times and clear a path for the soldiers advancing in his wake. Once through the Losheim Gap, he was to speed westward, taking all the villages and strongholds in his way until he captured the distant towns Stavelot and Trois Ponts. Once past Trois Ponts, Peiper would have a northwest dash of about twenty-five miles (40 km) to the Meuse.

Honsfeld, located about seven miles (11.2 km) from the Siegfried Line, was captured early on Day Two. With his tanks beginning to run low on fuel, Peiper swung north a short distance to a major American supply dump. He routed its few guards by noontime, grabbed fifty thousand gallons of gasoline, and took aim on his next target, the town of Ligneuville.

He now split his force into two groups. The first group, which was placed under the command of Major Josef Diefenthal, struck out for the town along a northerly route. Peiper himself led the second group along a southward course. His plan was to hit Ligneuville from two sides. It was a plan that worked well. The town fell in the afternoon. By 5:00 P.M., Peiper was clear of Ligneuville and plunging west.

The Malmedy Massacre

In the hours just before Ligneuville was reached, the group under Major Diefenthal committed one of the most atrocious acts in the battle history of World War II. It was an act that has been long remembered as the Malmedy Massacre.

While clanking through the woods near the village of Malmedy, Diefenthal's tanks ran into the 285th Field Artillery Observation Battalion, a unit belonging to the U.S. Ninth Army's 7th Armored Division. The 7th was just coming in from the north to help and the 285th was among the first of its units to arrive. Since its job was to watch the 7th's artillery fire and help the gunners zero in on their targets, the Battalion carried no heavy guns of its own. It had no choice but to surrender.

One hundred and twenty of the Battalion's men were herded into an open field. As they stood prisoner there, their German captors surrounded them and opened fire with machine guns. In all, eighty-five Americans were murdered on the spot before Deifenthal moved on. Their fellow soldiers escaped by throwing themselves to the ground and pretending to be dead.

The men of the 285th were not the only American prisoners to be killed in the Battle of the Bulge. Prisoners were shot at other captured spots. But when the bodies at Malmedy were later found by their 7th Division comrades, the news outraged the American forces everywhere and stiffened even more the already stiff United States defense.

Battlegroup Peiper Defeated

After capturing Ligneuville, Peiper spent the next two days advancing on and attacking Stavelot and Trois Ponts. He ran into trouble at both places. Before he could take Stavelot, he had to put up with thirteen stubborn soldiers from the 291st Combat Engineers Battalion. They buried land mines along the road into town and, with their single bazooka, destroyed his lead tank as it approached. Thirteen long hours passed before Battlegroup Peiper edged past the thirteen Americans. Next, at Trois Ponts, the force was delayed by engineers who dynamited three bridges across the city's Salm and Ambleve Rivers.

These delays proved fatal to Peiper. They gave the Americans time to move two divisions in against him before he got too close to the Meuse. The 82nd Airborne and the 30th Infantry Divisions attacked and retook Stavelot on December 19. Their victory cut Peiper's lead tanks from his supplies in the rear. He tried to press on, but the two divisions now hit him so hard with infantry attacks and artillery barrages that he lost men and equipment every step of the way. On December 23, Peiper faced the hard fact that he was almost out of fuel and that his force was all but destroyed. He ordered his men to abandon their tanks and retreat to safety.

With that order, the role of Battlegroup Peiper in the offensive came to a dismal end.

ACTION 3:
THE ATTACK ON ST. VITH

On the central sector of the front, General Manteuffel's Fifth Panzer Army made good gains on Day Two and then Day Three, December 18. In one of his areas, Manteuffel captured his first target, the village of Schoenberg, located just over five miles (8 km) from the Siegfried Line. As planned, the victory saw the 106th Division completely surrounded. Between eight thousand and nine thousand Americans were forced to lay down their arms.

With the 106th out of the battle, Manteuffel charged along the six miles (9.6 km) leading to the town of St. Vith and the major roadways running from it to the west, north, and south. But United States units rushed to the town's aid as he approached. The 7th Armored Division, which had lost its 285th Field Artillery Observation Battalion at Malmedy, was among the first on the scene. The new arrivals began to throw up a defensive line around three sides of St. Vith. The line was in the shape of a horseshoe, with the open end facing west.

When Manteuffel learned of the defensive line, he decided to have his forward troops bypass St. Vith to the north and south and continue pushing westward. The units coming up from behind were to attack the defensive line and capture the town.

Manteuffel began poking at the line but did not launch a full attack on St. Vith for several days. When the attack finally came on December 21, the little general was helped by several units from the Sixth SS Panzer Army. They had been transferred to him as soon as the German high command had realized that General Dietrich was stopped for good at Elsenborn Ridge. With them came the order that Manteuffel's army was now to lead the offensive.

As they knew would be the case, the American troops found themselves far outnumbered by the enemy when the attack began. Fighting in a falling snow and up against a massive tank, infantry, and artillery attack, their line began to crack in several spots. In one area, a small United States force was first battered by a long artillery barrage and then surrounded. The commander tried to sneak his men through the enemy circle when night fell. But the snow kept them from moving swiftly. They were soon taken prisoner.

The attack continued through the night and into December 22, with the Germans now pouring through holes along the line and closing in on the town. Knowing that St. Vith was lost, the Americans decided to leave and join a major defensive line being formed by General Hodges' U.S. First Army along the northern border of the front. But they hesitated. The battle had turned the snow to heavy mud. The retreating soldiers would be forced to move with agonizing slowness and would be easy targets for the enemy artillery.

And so the defenders held on through another night. Fortunately, the hours of darkness brought a sudden frost that hardened the ground. Just before the dawn of December 23, the Americans were pulling out in swift and orderly fashion and heading northwest to the new defensive line. Manteuffel's tanks and infantry entered St. Vith.

ACTION 4:
THE TAKING OF HOUFFALIZE

The town of Houffalize, located southwest of St. Vith and a little over twelve miles (19 km) from the Siegfried Line, was another of Manteuffel's targets. His advance on the town saw his heavy forces push steadily ahead in the face of stiff resistance. Houffalize was in German hands by December 20, the victim of a combined tank and infantry attack.

ACTION 5:
THE ATTACK ON BASTOGNE

Near the southern end of Manteuffel's area, his troops charged toward Clervaux on Day One. Standing some five miles (8 km) inside the American lines, the town fell to him on Day Two after he had beaten off a small but sharp counterattack. From there, his forces spread out in three directions. Some swung northwest to help take Houffalize. The others moved west and were joined by units from General Brandenberger's Seventh Army.

The troops knifing west had their sights set on an objective twenty-five miles (40 km) away. It was one of the offensive's most vital targets—the city of Bastogne. It was needed because seven main roadways, each useful for the quick movement of men and supplies, stretched away from it in all directions. Autumn Fog called for the infantry, backed by some tank outfits, to capture Bastogne. Simultaneously, a major tank force was to bypass it to the north and south and continue westward.

Bastogne was manned by a few units from the 9th Armored Division. Knowing that they would soon be attacked, their commander placed them in defensive positions in the path of the approaching enemy. They were soon joined by some of the troops that General Eisenhower had summoned on first hearing of the offensive. Outfits from the 10th Armored Division, which had been sent from General George Patton's Third Army in France, arrived first, with the 101st Airborne Division coming close behind. Soon established was a defensive line that arced around Bastogne's northern, eastern, and southern sides.

The first German tanks and infantry reached the line on December 19 and began probing for weak spots. It broke at one point when a small defending unit was overwhelmed and forced to retreat; tanks caught the unit in the open some minutes later and wiped it out. But, close by, the 501st Parachute Infantry Regiment of the 101st Airborne pushed the enemy back and closed the break. To the south of the city, another 101st regiment—the 506th Parachute Infantry—beat off a tank attack. The result of the probes made one fact clear to the Germans: The line was going to be hard to breach.

As the day's fighting ended, two German tank divisions prepared themselves to bypass Bastogne and thrust westward. They were the 2nd Panzer Division and an outfit known as the Panzer *Lehr*. The commander in charge of taking the city itself wondered how best to break through the defensive line.

A Major Development

December 19 also saw a major development far to Bastogne's south. In France, General Eisenhower met with his top commanders and decided on a plan to crush the offensive. The plan called for American forces to press in on the Germans from the north, south, and west and then push them eastward back across the Siegfried Line. The First Army under General Hodges would handle matters from the north and west.

Some of his troops were already in the fighting. Others were moving into place along a defensive line at the northern edge of the Ardennes (the line that the defenders of St. Vith would head for on December 23). Hodges would launch his push against the Germans from this line.

For the campaign from the south, Eisenhower turned to General Patton. Patton, with his 10th Armored Division already in the Ardennes, was now ordered to bring the rest of his Third Army up from France as fast as possible. At the moment, working side by side with the Seventh Army, Patton's men were attacking Germany's industrial Saar area. That attack was to be left to the Seventh.

Bastogne immediately showed itself to be vital to the campaign from the south. Patton was to divide his army into two forces. They were to be called Combat Commands A and B (CCA and CCB). On spearing into the Ardennes, they would split the forward German troops from those in the rear and thus break the enemy's flow of supplies. The split would be accomplished by having CCA slam into Bastogne while CCB struck to the east of the city. The two forces would then widen the split—fatally for the Germans—by attacking north and east.

Every man at the meeting knew that Bastogne must not now be allowed to fall into enemy hands. If it did, the costs of retaking it would be terrible. Hundreds of lives would be lost and the already difficult job of crushing the offensive would be made even harder.

But there was a terrible question: Could Bastogne's troops, badly outnumbered and enduring snowy weather that kept Allied planes from dropping needed supplies on the city, hold out for the several days that Patton would need to move the Third Army into the Ardennes? The next days would answer that question.

Bastogne Under Attack

At Bastogne, the 101st Airborne Division was under the temporary command of Brigadier General Anthony McAuliffe

The cold, snowy weather of late December made fighting even more difficult for U.S. troops in the Ardennes.

because the division's commander, Major General Maxwell Taylor, had gone home to the United States on leave just before the offensive opened. McAuliffe, who was the division's top artillery officer, was now placed in command of all troops defending the city.

On December 20, the German attackers continued their probes of the line, with a number of their forces swinging around both sides of Bastogne and completely surrounding the city. For his part, McAuliffe shifted certain of his units, tightening the defenses around Bastogne, and preparing himself for the all-out attack that would certainly come in a matter of hours. At day's end, McAuliffe could view his situation with mixed feelings.

On the one hand, he had his troops well positioned to defend the city. Though outnumbered, he had a solid force of good men—four regiments of the 101st (three parachute regiments and one glider regiment), four light artillery units, two medium howitzer outfits, an armored field artillery battalion, and a tank destroyer battalion. His artillery pieces numbered forty.

On the other hand, he was running desperately low on ammunition—and could expect none until the weather cleared and made an airdrop possible. Should he run out of fire power, it would not matter how good his men were as fighters or how well they were positioned. The need for ammunition grew so great in the next days that three tanks and two half-track vehicles tried to break through the German encirclement. Their hope was to locate friendly troops and return with a cargo of shells and bullets. They were quickly sighted and destroyed.

From December 19 to 22, the Germans continued to smash into the defensive line. They were successfully repulsed at all but one point, where they broke through only to be stopped a short distance later. On December 22, General Heinz Kokott, the officer charged with taking Bastogne, received special instructions from the German high command. The high command had learned that the U.S. Third

Army was on the march from the south. Kokott was ordered to lose no more time on attacks but to try for a quick surrender before the Third arrived.

Accordingly, he sent four men—two officers and two enlisted men—into the American lines with a message for McAuliffe. It informed McAuliffe that he was surrounded by a superior force, that he faced certain defeat, that lives would be wasted if he continued the fight, and that he now should bow to the inevitable and surrender.

Carrying a white flag to indicate that they came in peace, the four entered the United States lines. They were sighted and taken to a nearby command post. Their message was quickly telephoned to McAuliffe in Bastogne. They waited for his reply.

When it came, McAuliffe's written answer was a defiant one-word message that won him fame throughout the western world. Ever since, it has ranked as one of the most unusual communiques in military history. McAuliffe wrote:

"Nuts."

Though the reply rang with confidence, McAuliffe's position was growing more desperate with each passing hour. His ammunition had run so low that his artillery pieces were rationed to ten shells each per day. Fortunately, the weather cleared on December 23 and 24, enabling air drops that brought in much-needed supplies, plus air attacks on the surrounding German units. But the weather closed down again late Christmas Eve and the help from the air ceased.

In the meantime, Patton's Third Army was slashing up from the south and, though meeting heavy resistance, was expected to arrive in another day or so. General Kokott, with the bid for a quick surrender having failed and with Patton fast approaching, turned back to battle tactics. On Christmas Day, he launched a major effort to take the city.

At 3:00 A.M. that day, he sent a regiment on the attack northwest of the city. Its aim was to tie down the Americans there while a tank-and-infantry force broke through and smashed into Bastogne itself. By dawn, the strategy seemed to be working. The tank-and-infantry unit was pouring through the defensive line and charging toward the city.

But then the picture suddenly changed—with tragic consequences for the attackers. They plunged into a trap that had been set by the Americans. Well-placed troopers with the 501st Parachute Infantry Regiment began picking off the German infantrymen. Bastogne's single tank destroyer battalion opened fire on the tanks. The attack came to a halt and the Germans fled, leaving behind seventeen destroyed tanks. Kokott's last chance to take Bastogne had ended in failure.

Meanwhile, the Third Army's CCA and CCB, though meeting a desperate enemy resistance, were steadily approaching. CCA, which had the job of entering Bastogne itself, fought its way to the nearby town of Reconville by Christmas Day. The entire day was given to taking the town. The battle was won late in the afternoon. CCA began pouring along a main road to Bastogne. Twenty-four hours later, its men smashed into the village of Assenois, which lay at the edge of Bastogne's defensive line. Minutes later, they were being welcomed by the city's defenders. To the east, CCB was hitting behind General Kokott's troops.

The question of whether the defenders of Bastogne could hold out until help arrived had been answered.

THE TIDE TURNS

The five German actions that have brought us to this point in the chapter led to three final actions.

The three actions, which are shown on the facing map, were launched on December 21. Each met with defeat as the tide of battle now turned in the Americans' favor. The first saw the German troops that had bypassed St. Vith (soon joined by those that had taken the city) attack northwest. After advancing a few miles, they were stopped at the defensive line that the First Army had formed along the northern edge of the Ardennes. Likewise, the forces that had taken

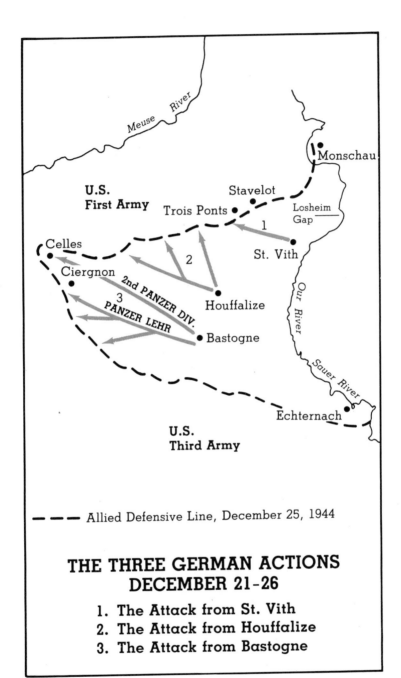

THE THREE GERMAN ACTIONS
DECEMBER 21-26

1. The Attack from St. Vith
2. The Attack from Houffalize
3. The Attack from Bastogne

Houffalize headed northwest. They, too, were halted at the defensive line.

After bypassing Bastogne, the 2nd Panzer Division and the Panzer *Lehr* attacked west with great success for a time. They pounded through light defenses, with the 2nd Panzer making the offensive's deepest penetration into Belgium. Its tanks roared into the town of Celles on Christmas Day. Celles stood a mere four miles (6.4 km) from the Meuse.

Quickly pushing on, the 2nd Panzer ran into the 2nd Armored Division from the First Army. A battle, consisting of dozens of individual fights, erupted and lasted through the night. It ended the next day in disaster for the Germans. Though elements from the Panzer *Lehr* tried to come to its aid, the 2nd Panzer was demolished. Its losses included 2500 men killed or wounded, 1200 taken prisoner, and 405 vehicles (including eighty-eight tanks) destroyed or captured. The Panzer *Lehr*, which had been following a course to the 2nd's south, tried to battle on, but was eventually called back to the east to fight when the U.S. First and Third Armies—with strong British and Canadian help—began to drive the Germans out of Belgium.

With the 2nd's defeat, the offensive was smashed for good. Long days of fighting remained, but they were days that saw the Allies steadily push the once proud and eager but now exhausted German troops back toward the Siegfried Line.

By January 2, 1945, the Germans had their backs against an arcing line that ran from below Stavelot in the north to a point some fifteen miles (24 km) east of Celles and on to a spot about five miles (8 km) east of Bastogne. By mid-month, the German line stretched down past St. Vith in the north to Houffalize and then to the town of Wiltz. Early February saw the Germans retreating across the Siegfried Line at all points along the front.

One of the most decisive of all the war's battles was at an end. It was a battle that had exacted a terrible toll in property, equipment, and, worst of all, human life. Towns and cities

Infantrymen of the 2nd SS Panzer Division fight their way across a road blocked by American vehicles.

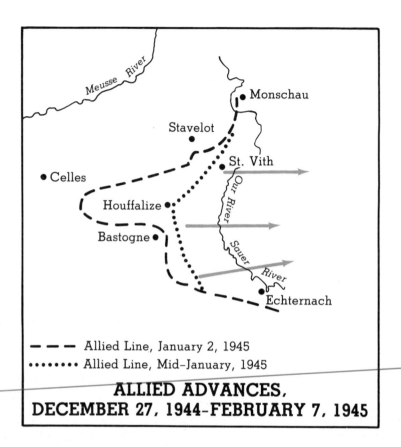

— — — Allied Line, January 2, 1945

•••••• Allied Line, Mid–January, 1945

ALLIED ADVANCES,
DECEMBER 27, 1944–FEBRUARY 7, 1945

such as Bastogne and St. Vith lay in ruins, with many of their people homeless and huddled for safety in the basements of churches and public buildings. Millions of dollars in equipment had been destroyed. And the awful cost in death and injury totaled more than 195,000 soldiers.

The Americans suffered more than 75,000 casualties. Of that number, 8497 were known to have died; 46,000 had been wounded; and some 21,000 were missing or in enemy prisoner-of-war camps.

German casualties were far more terrible. They added up to nearly 120,000 men. Listed as killed were 12,652. Some

*Flanked by Reich Marshal Hermann Goering (left)
and General Heinz Guderian, Hitler reviews the Germans'
position in the Ardennes on New Year's Day, 1945.*

57,000 were reported as injured. About 50,000 had been captured.

As for Hitler, his dream of a miracle victory and a swift ending of the war in his favor had turned into a nightmare that had sacrificed the very finest of his fighting men. His doom—and that of his Germany—was sealed.

CHAPTER

YALTA AND
THE UNITED NATIONS

In early February, 1945, the last of the German invaders were being driven out of the Ardennes. To the south, Allied units had advanced into Germany from France and were moving on the Rhine River, beyond which lay the very heart of the enemy nation. To the east, Soviet troops had just freed all of Poland and were now battling to get across the Oder River on the German side of the German-Polish border. They were just some forty miles (64 km) from their ultimate target—Hitler's capital city, Berlin.

Despite the fierce fighting on the various fronts, the world turned its attention from the news of battles for eight days early in the month. All eyes went to a city in southern Russia.

The city, located alongside the Black Sea, was Yalta. It stood on the Crimea peninsula, which Hitler had grabbed in the early days of his Russian invasion. It had been the scene of bloody fighting in 1944 when the Russians had driven his forces back out. Here, in a former resort city, the leaders of the Allied nations known as "The Big Three" met to decide on matters that would affect the postwar world for decades to come. They knew that Germany's final defeat was just weeks away.

The three were President Franklin D. Roosevelt of the United States, Prime Minister Winston Churchill of Great Britain, and Marshal Joseph Stalin of the Soviet Union.

Their meetings, which were held from February 4 to 11, would go down in the history of the war as the Yalta Conference. At the time, it was also known as the Argonaut Conference, with the name referring to the sailors who, in Greek mythology, sailed out so courageously to find the priceless Golden Fleece.

WHAT HAD GONE BEFORE

As historic as it was, the Yalta Conference did not mark the first time that the Allied nations, in one combination or another, had convened for talks. For example, four major conversations had been held in 1943. They had begun in August when Roosevelt and Churchill met in Quebec, Canada, with a Chinese delegation. The purpose of the session had been to make plans for the war against Japan.

The following October had seen representatives from the United States, Great Britain, and the Soviet Union gather in Moscow. The result had been the issuance of a declaration in which the three countries pledged to cooperate not only in carrying out the war but also in maintaining international peace after the fighting ended. Though China did not have representatives at the meeting, it joined in the declaration.

One month later, President Roosevelt and Prime Minister Churchill traveled to Cairo, Egypt, for a meeting with the head of the Chinese government, Generalissimo Chiang Kai-shek. As had been the case earlier at Quebec, the military strategies to be employed against Japan were discussed. From Cairo, Roosevelt and Churchill went directly to the city of Teheran (located in what was called Persia at the time, and is now Iran), where they were joined by Stalin. The three talked over plans for the final destruction of the German army and issued a statement saying that they would work together for world peace when the fighting ended.

In their statement, they extended an invitation to all countries to join a "world family of democratic nations." This "family" was to emerge a few months later as the international body, the United Nations. More would be done on the organization's behalf at the Yalta Conference, and it would take shape soon thereafter.

THE "BIG THREE"
LEADERS

And now, in February, 1945, the three leaders were meeting at the ornate Livadia Palace just outside Yalta. Roosevelt and Churchill had come to the conference by sea, while Stalin had traveled down from Moscow by train. The three were all in their sixties and were all master politicians and experienced statesmen. Churchill, aged sixty-nine, was the oldest of the trio.

Winston Churchill

Born to an aristocratic family on November 30, 1874, Churchill had spent his early years as an army officer and newspaper correspondent. First elected to the British Parliament in 1901, he served as First Lord of the Admiralty (the official in charge of the Navy) from 1911 to 1915, after which he served in various government posts until 1929. During the 1930s, he continually warned the British government of the dangers of war posed by Hitler and urged a buildup of the nation's armed forces. His words went unheeded by a government that, with the terrible loss of British life in the First World War still in mind, wanted to avoid an armed confrontation with Germany.

When the government finally declared war in 1939, Churchill was again named First Lord of the Admiralty. He became Prime Minister in 1940 and had served in that capacity ever since, lifting the morale of his people with his leadership—especially during the Battle of Britain—and inspiring them with his bulldog looks and his bulldoglike determination to see Hitler's Germany crushed.

Joseph Stalin

Aged sixty-five and small in stature—he stood just five feet six inches tall—Stalin was the next oldest. The son of a shoemaker in the Russian state of Georgia, he planned to be a priest, but became interested in Marxism and entered politics instead. He participated in the revolution that overthrew the Russian royal family in 1917, took the country out of World War I, and gave her a communist government. Rising rapidly in politics, Stalin was elected General Secretary of the Russian Communist Party in 1922 and became the dictatorial head of the Soviet Union in 1929, a position that he was to hold until his death in 1953.

As you'll recall, Stalin signed a nonaggression pact with Hitler in 1939 and joined his fellow dictator in the attack on Poland. He switched to the Allied side when Hitler discarded the pact and invaded Russia in 1941.

Franklin D. Roosevelt

Born January 30, 1882, Roosevelt celebrated his sixty-third birthday just before arriving at Yalta. The son of wealthy and socially prominent parents, he won his first political post in 1910 when he was elected as a Democrat to the New York State Senate. He was appointed Assistant Secretary of the Navy in 1913 and held the position until 1921.

That year of 1921 saw Roosevelt suffer a polio attack that left him crippled and unable to walk without the support of leg braces for the rest of his life. Despite his handicap, Roosevelt returned to politics in 1924, twice serving as the governor of New York State and then advancing to the White House in 1933. After working with much success to bring the United States out of the Great Depression, Roosevelt led the nation through the war years. He was elected to an unprecedented fourth term as president in 1944.

At the time of the Yalta Conference, the strains of his many years in the White House had weakened Roosevelt. He was a desperately ill man with just a few weeks left to live.

THE YALTA AGREEMENTS

Flanked by their advisers and aides, the three leaders sat down at a table in Livadia Palace and hammered out a series

The "Big Three" at Yalta (seated from left):
Prime Minister Winston S. Churchill,
President Franklin D. Roosevelt,
and Marshal Joseph Stalin.

of far-reaching agreements. Those agreements concerned the following issues:

Defeated Germany

The three agreed that nothing less than unconditional surrender was to be required of Hitler. Once defeated, Germany was to be occupied and policed by American, British, and Russian troops. The country was to be divided into zones, with one being assigned to each of the occupying powers. France was to be invited to take a zone if she so desired. The entire occupation was to be supervised by a central control commission manned by representatives of the Allied nations involved.

In great part, the invitation to France was extended out of courtesy. Because she had fallen to Hitler in 1940, she had not been able to do as much in the war as her fellow Allied nations. She had, however, fought valiantly on being freed by the D-Day forces in 1944. Her troops were commanded by General Charles de Gaulle, who had gone to Great Britain on Hitler's approach and had established the Free French government there. His forces were first made up of men who managed to escape the German yoke and then of those freed in 1944. When the D-Day troops made their way inland and captured Paris, de Gaulle took control of liberated France and did much to restore her people's morale and pride. He would later serve twice as the nation's president.

The invitation was also issued much at Winston Churchill's urging, though wise statesman that he was, he never voiced his opinion to Stalin. Churchill feared that the dictator would turn the Russian zone into a communist area. With France acting as one of the occupying powers, there would be four zones rather than three. Russia would thus receive a smaller zone and would be able to bring communism to bear upon fewer people. Churchill was delighted when France later accepted the invitation.

The agreement concerning Germany contained three further provisions. First, reparations (moneys exacted for the damages done in the war) were to be collected from the nation; when their exact amounts were determined, Russia was to receive the lion's share, in great part because she had lost the most men in the fighting. Second, Germany's war industries were to be eliminated. Finally, the most barbarous of her leaders were to be brought to trial as war criminals.

The Liberated People
of Europe

The three said that, once the countries that had been held captive by Germany were set free, they would be given help in destroying the last vestiges of Hitler's Nazism within their borders. They were also to be assisted in establishing governments of their choice through free elections. Italy and the small countries that had sided with the Axis were to be made to pay reparations.

A New Poland

Stalin, you'll remember, had joined Hitler's 1939 invasion of Poland and had taken the western area of the country. He had been driven back out in 1941 when Hitler, discarding their nonaggression pact, had sent troops blasting through Poland as part of his invasion of Russia. Just recently, as the Russians stormed toward Germany, they had reentered Poland and had wrested all of the nation from Nazi hands. The advance on Germany had also seen Stalin's troops, in 1944, overrun three Eastern European countries that had sided with Hitler—Hungary, Rumania, and Bulgaria.

With his armies holding as much of Eastern Europe as they did, Stalin now wanted to secure his power base there so that the area would fall completely under his control once and for all. So he bargained with Roosevelt and Churchill to have the Baltic countries to Poland's north placed in his domain. They were Estonia, Latvia, and Lithuania. Lithuania had earlier been a Russian state.

To get all that he wanted, Stalin also entered a special agreement concerning Poland itself. Though he now held the country militarily and could have imposed on it his own dictatorship, he agreed that Poland was to be treated like the other once-captive nations. Her people would be allowed to establish a government of their own choosing through a free election. In return, he was to be awarded a portion of East Prussia, the German area on the northern Polish border. Poland herself was to be compensated in part for the German-Soviet invasion of 1939 by receiving the remainder of East Prussia.

Stalin's every demand was met and the political and geographical maps of Eastern Europe were changed into what they are today. He later sidestepped his promise to give Poland a government of her own choosing. In 1947, when the time came to form that government, his communist followers dominated the elections. Since then, Poland has been a Soviet-dominated state. Similar fates befell the other Eastern European countries—Hungary, Rumania, and Bulgaria all fell within the Soviet sphere. Estonia, Latvia, and Lithuania were made states within the Soviet Union.

The Far East

Mr. Roosevelt was deeply worried about the Japanese war when he came to Yalta. The atomic bomb was under development at the time, but he had no idea that it would soon be ready for use and would, later in this very year of 1945, bring the Pacific conflict to an abrupt close when dropped on the Japanese cities of Hiroshima and Nagasaki. What he knew was that current United States plans called for an invasion of the Japanese home islands. Estimates held that the invasion would cost the American forces more than a million men killed, wounded, or missing in action.

Consequently, the president was eager for assistance and wanted Stalin, who had never declared war on Japan, to lend a hand with the invasion. Specifically, he hoped to have Russia attack the Japanese forces in Korea and China's Manchuria, tying them down so that they could not come to the assistance of the beleaguered homeland. It was a tactic bound to shorten the home island fighting and save countless American lives.

Stalin agreed to go to war against Japan within two or three months after the collapse of Germany. But he struck a hard bargain for his cooperation. In return, he had Roosevelt agree that Russia would be given:

- The Japanese Kurile Islands. A chain of fifty-six volcanic islands, they form an arc between Japan's northernmost island—Hokkaido—and Russia's Kamchatka Peninsula.

- The southern half of Sakhalin Island. A long and narrow island just off the Soviet eastern coast, Sakhalin had been lost by the Russians to the Japanese during a war in 1905.

- Special privileges at Port Arthur and the city of Dairen. Both are on the China coast near the border with Korea.

- Joint control (with China) of the railroads in China's Manchuria.

These agreements, which led to Stalin's declaration of war against Japan on August 9, 1945, gave Russia great power in the Far East. They proved to be agreements that caused widespread controversy.

For years to come, Roosevelt was sharply criticized on several counts by many people across the world. First, they said that he need not have made the agreements in the first place. Stalin had gone to war against Japan three days after the atomic bomb had been dropped on Hiroshima. The bomb had ended the Pacific fighting with breathtaking suddenness, and his help against the Japanese had turned out to be unnecessary. Further, Roosevelt's critics charged that Stalin would have come into Pacific conflict anyway, just to take whatever spoils of war he could grab. It had been needless to hand him all that Far Eastern power just to get him into the fighting.

Roosevelt's critics also charged that, in giving the Soviets so much power, he had betrayed his Chinese ally, Generalissimo Chiang Kai-chek, who had been fighting the Japanese since the 1930s. They argued that the President had weakened the Generalissimo's political strength at home and had damaged the morale of his supporters. At the time, Chiang's government was beset by communist factions in the country. Four years later, he was overthrown and China was given a communist government, a government that has remained in power to this day.

Many people felt that Roosevelt's failing health had been behind the Far Eastern agreements. He had been too sick, they contended, to bargain wisely and strongly with Stalin.

But the President had his share of supporters. They argued that, without the agreements, Stalin and his giant armies could have taken far more power in China at the close of the Pacific fighting. The agreements, which he honored in great part, had put a definite rein on the dictator's Far Eastern ambitions.

A World Organization

On a happier note, the three leaders cleared the way for the establishment of an international body dedicated to preserving the world's peace and security. They did so by calling for a multination conference to be held as soon as possible in San Francisco, California. Its purpose would be to draw up a charter for the organization that would be known as the United Nations.

With the way paved for the formation of a body meant to help keep future international disputes from exploding into a new world war, the three leaders went their separate ways, each returning to his own country. The "Big Three" powers would convene once more in the months following Germany's defeat. But Roosevelt, Churchill, and Stalin would never again meet as a group. Roosevelt would die of a cerebral hemorrhage in almost exactly two months. The British people, though appreciating and admiring Churchill's wartime leadership, would vote his political party out of office soon after war's end, and replace his government with one they thought would suit them better in peacetime.

THE UNITED NATIONS

The term "United Nations" was coined by President Roosevelt early in the war. He had meant it to designate all the countries fighting the Axis Powers. It was now to become the name of the international peacekeeping organization.

The idea for such an organization was not new. In the wake of World War I, a similar body—the League of Nations—had taken shape. Due mainly to international rivalries and suspicions within its ranks, it had failed in its mission to preserve world order and harmony. Despite that failure, the allied nations in World War II agreed that they must try again and form a new League, whatever its name might prove to be, when peace returned.

The four meetings held by the Allied nations in 1943 all ended with declarations favoring the formation of such a body. For example, the United States, British, and Soviet representatives who met at Moscow in October of that year announced that they recognized "the necessity of establishing at the earliest practicable date a general international organization based upon the principle of the sovereign equality of all peace-loving states, large and small, for the maintenance of international peace and security." Later, as you know, Roosevelt, Churchill, and Stalin had closed their Teheran meeting with an invitation to all countries to join a "world family of democratic nations."

The first actual step toward the formation of this "family" was taken in 1944. From August 21 to October 7, representatives from the United States, Great Britain, Russia, and China sat down together at Dumbarton Oaks, an old mansion located in Washington, D.C. They fashioned a framework for an organization that would see the countries now fighting the Axis remain united in peacetime so that they could work for an orderly and cooperative world.

Their ideas were known as the Dumbarton Oaks Proposals. The Proposals went on to serve as guides for the delegates who brought the United Nations into being at the San Francisco Conference.

The Conference, called one of the most important in history, opened on April 25, 1945, with delegates from forty-six nations in attendance. While a light rain fell outside, they gathered in the city's War Memorial Opera House. There, in a span of three months, they fashioned the United Nations Charter, the document stating the organization's principles, its structure, and its rules of operation.

Upon its completion in late July, the Charter was signed by fifty-one nations. Launched was the organization that today, though often beset with strife, continues the work of trying to solve the world's problems without bloodshed. At present, that work is being carried on at the United Nations headquarters in New York City by 159 member nations.

As the delegates to the San Francisco Conference were seeking an orderly and harmonious future, the war in Europe was writing its final pages. They are pages that now take us back to February, 1945.